EXTREME PUMPKINS II

Take Back Halloween and Freak Out a Few More Neighbors

TOM NARDONE
Author of the national bestseller EXTREME PUMPKINS

HOME

A HOME BOOK
Published by the Penguin Group
Penguin Group (USA) Inc.
375 Hudson Street, New York, New York 10014, USA

Penguin Group (Canada), 90 Eglinton Avenue East, Suite 700,
Toronto, Ontario M4P 2Y3, Canada
(a division of Pearson Penguin Canada Inc.)

Penguin Books ltda., 80 Strand, London WC2R 0RL, England

Penguin Group Ireland, 25 St. Stephen's Green, Dublin 2, Ireland
(a division of Penguin Books Ltd.)

Penguin Group (Australia), 250 Camberwell Road, Camberwell,
Victoria 3124, Australia
(a division of Pearson Australia Group Pty. Ltd.)

Penguin Books India Pvt. Ltd., 11 Community Centre,
Panchsheel Park, New Delhi—110 017, India

Penguin Group (NZ), 67 Apollo Drive, Rosedale,
North Shore 0632, New Zealand
(a division of Pearson New Zealand Ltd.)

Penguin Books (South Africa) (Pty.) Ltd., 24 Sturdee Avenue,
Rosebank, Johannesburg 2196, South Africa

Penguin Books Ltd., Registered Offices: 80 Strand,
London WC2R 0RL, England

While the author has made every effort to provide accurate telephone
numbers and Internet addresses at the time of publication, neither the
publisher nor the author assumes any responsibility for errors, or for
changes that occur after publication. Further, the publisher does not
have any control over and does not assume any responsibility for author
or third-party websites or their content.

A QUIRK PACKAGING BOOK
Copyright © 2008 by Quirk Packaging, Inc.
Photography by Tom Nardone
Designed by Sue Livingston
Developmental editing by Sarah Scheffel
Line editing by Jennifer Boudinot
Illustrations by Nancy Leonard

First edition: September 2008

Library of Congress Cataloging-in-Publication Data

Nardone, Tom.
  Extreme pumpkins II : take back Halloween and freak out a few more
neighbors / Tom Nardone. — 1st ed.
    p. cm.
  Includes index.
  ISBN 978-1-55788-533-3
  1. Halloween decorations. 2. Handicraft. I. Title.
  TT900.H32N372 2008
  745.594'1646—dc22
                                        2008005585

Printed in the United States of America

10   9   8   7   6   5   4

Most Home books are available at special quantity discounts for bulk
purchases for sales promotions, premiums, fund-raising, or educational
use. Special books, or book excerpts, can also be created to fit specific
needs. For details, write: Special Markets, Penguin Group (USA) Inc., 375
Hudson Street, New York, New York 10014.

DISCLAIMER

THIS BOOK IS NOT INTENDED FOR CHILDREN.
The projects described in this book should be done only by
adults or by older children under close adult supervision.

SAFETY FIRST: Safety should be your top priority. If you're
careless, you could get injured. The publisher, author, and
packager of this book do not claim that the information
contained herein is complete or accurate for your specific
situation. It should by no means be considered a substitute for good judgment, skill, and common sense. In addi-
tion, neither the publisher, author, nor packager endorses
or encourages any irresponsible behavior, and specifically
disclaims responsibility for any liability, loss, damage, or
injury allegedly arising from any suggestion, information,
or instruction in this book. We urge you to obey the law
and the dictates of common sense at all times.

CONTENTS

EXTREME PUMPKIN DESIGN MANIFESTO

My hope is that *Extreme Pumpkins II* will give you some extremely gross, tasteless, scary pumpkin-carving ideas, or at least lots of cool things to copy. And if you hate this book, well, maybe that will inspire you too.

THINGS I HATE	WHAT I DO INSTEAD
Cutesy pumpkins with painted-on faces	Hack up pumpkins so their faces are repulsive (see page 72)
Safetycrats who take all of the glee out of life	Remind people that flying pumpkin guts can be fun (see page 20)
Sickeningly sweet fairytales	Create pumpkin designs sure to disillusion those who buy into these smarmy tales (see page 80)
Wasting time on a craft project	Use power tools to carve pumpkins in a nanosecond (see page 30)
Perfectionism	Use power tools with my eyes closed (Just kidding!)
Out-of-control toddlers	Create a pumpkin parody (see page 12)
People who think pumpkin carving is a high art	Show everyone how easy (and truly low brow) pumpkin carving can be (see page 84)
Nicey-nice neighbors	Create a pumpkin head on a spike as a welcome wagon (see page 68)
Monotony	Try new gnarly designs, even when they fail miserably (see Beware box, page 9)
Pumpkins based on Disney characters	Dream up pumpkins based on horror film characters (see pages 24, 60, 64, and 88)
Over-age trick-or-treaters	Do you own a garden hose? (For more ideas, see Punk Alert box, page 59)
The feeling of not accomplishing anything	Make something, anything, because even the most useless thing is better than nothing (see page 60)
Changing babies' diapers	Create a pumpkin-pulp interpretation (see page 76)
Good manners	Carve designs so rude I offend myself (see page 84)

INTRODUCTION

Welcome to *Extreme Pumpkins II,* or as I like to call it, *Son of Extreme Pumpkins*. Like most gross, violent, kitschy blockbuster horror films, my first book, *Extreme Pumpkins,* has spawned a sequel. And, like any truly horrifying sequel, *Extreme Pumpkins II* is even more tasteless, terrifying, and outrageous than the first book. I've come up with 20 all-new extreme pumpkin designs that will make Puking Pumpkin look tasteful and the Cannibal Pumpkin look like kid stuff.

So, if you have the stomach for it, let's get started. I imagine you bought this book for the same reason I buy how-to books—to copy them. I find that copying other people's ideas is the best and by far the easiest way to get through life. I suggest you do the same. You paid for this book, so go right ahead and copy my pumpkin designs. If you want, you can even sign my name "Tom Nardone" on your jack-o'-lanterns. It'll be cool: I'll be like Andy Warhol with my own pop art factory churning out extreme pumpkins nationwide.

"But what if I want to design my own extreme pumpkins?" you ask. On the rare occasion that I can't find something worth copying, I follow my own personal design strategy, which I'll share with you now: If you can't find inspiration from other sources, find loathing. Begin by thinking very hard about all the stuff in the world you don't like. Focus on something you especially hate, and decide what is wrong with it. Then, make the exact opposite. For example, I especially dislike Thomas Kincaid paintings. His depictions of quaint little cottages with glowing highlights make me want to gag myself with a gravy ladle. So, if I were looking for a subject for a mural to paint, I would think of the opposites. Pin-ups and flaming hot-rod engines come to mind first, but I never rule out the presence of skulls in anything I do.

In other words, find something you hate, and then tap into your creativity to kick it in the teeth. Opposite is a chart of some things I hate and how they have fueled the extreme pumpkin designs featured here.

TOOLS FOR TERROR

When it's pumpkin-carving time, I use power tools. This isn't just because they make carving quick and I am lazy; power tools make it possible to cut out all sorts of really cool shapes and look cool while you're doing it. Below you'll find descriptions of the extreme pumpkin-carving tools I recommend, including the jigsaw, reciprocating saw, electric drill, router, and my two new favorites, the angle grinder and Dremel rotary tool. If you don't yet own these awesome tools of destruction, I suggest you visit your neighborhood hardware store and check them out. You won't come home empty-handed.

After my power tool overview, you'll find descriptions of some regular hand tools you can use instead, and still see extreme results. (See The Standard Toolbox: Alternatives to Power Tools, page 9.) If you're klutzy, you might want to go with the hand tools, since even the coolest extreme pumpkin on the block is not worth loss of life or limb. And, of course, kids and teens, however awesome, should never use power tools without adult supervision.

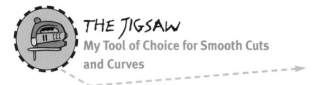

THE JIGSAW
My Tool of Choice for Smooth Cuts and Curves

If you're going to be stranded on a deserted island in October and can bring only one tool to carve pumpkins (or large tropical fruits), bring the jigsaw. Even the smallest jigsaw has plenty of power to slice and dice the soft flesh of a pumpkin. With a jigsaw, doing curves is way easier than with a kitchen knife, and it's quick, too. (Just don't go so fast you accidentally cut off something you need, like your thumb.) Jigsaws are such fantastic pumpkin-carving tools I think hardware stores should start marketing them as jack-o'-lantern saws.

- **GET THE LONGEST BLADE** *available for the most versatility. The one I normally use is 8 inches (20 cm).*

- **FOR MAXIMUM CONTROL,** *plunge the jigsaw blade into the pumpkin before you pull the trigger to turn it on. You don't want a runaway jigsaw wreaking havoc on your pumpkin (or your person).*

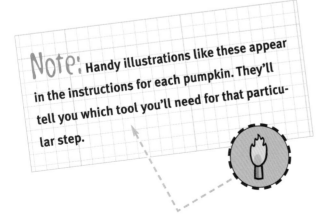

Note: Handy illustrations like these appear in the instructions for each pumpkin. They'll tell you which tool you'll need for that particular step.

- **TO KEEP THE JIGSAW STEADY,** *I recommend holding it in position with two hands. It's easy to overshoot your mark because the saw cuts through the pumpkin flesh so quickly; using two hands will help you control the saw more easily.*

THE RECIPROCATING SAW
The Bad Boy for Cutting Thick, Tough Flesh

If the jigsaw isn't man enough for you, meet the reciprocating saw. Unlike jigsaws, which have short blades, reciprocating saws can often handle blades of 10 or more inches (25 cm). If a blade that long can easily slice through a dead raccoon (and it can), it can easily slice through even the most ornery pumpkin. In fact, when you're working with a huge pumpkin that requires deep cuts, a recipro is a no-brainer. You can carve up a giant jack-o'-lantern in less time than it would take you to drive to the nearest Olive Garden and throw a chopped raccoon carcass in their Dumpster.

- **YOU NEED A RECIPROCATING SAW** *only when the pumpkin flesh is too thick for a jigsaw to carve with ease.*

- **RECIPROCATING SAWS ARE BIG TOOLS** *with a lot of power. This means they can be tricky to maneuver, so a) you may want to lift some weights before you attempt to steer one of these butt-kicking tools; and b) don't try to do really intricate designs when you're using the reciprocating saw. Attempt too many twists and curves and you're likely to end up with a heap of pumpkin pulp.*

THE ELECTRIC DRILL
The Go-to Tool for Poking out Eyes and Other Holes

Carving a circle with a jigsaw or knife is as tricky as making a circle on an Etch A Sketch. That's why my weapon of choice for gouging out eyes and poking holes in general is the electric drill. A drill will also come in handy when attaching pumpkin parts to one another using wood screws.

- **YOU'LL WANT A SELECTION** *of drill bits in a range of different sizes. Experiment and see what size works best for you. You also may want to drill holes of different sizes, such as when you want to make one eye bigger than the other.*

- **FOR LESS-PERFECT HOLES** *for those nastier pumpkins, try this: After you finish drilling the hole, while your drill bit is still inside the pumpkin, wobble the drill around to make the hole more uneven and mean-looking.*

THE ROUTER
The Original Flayer

I know I don't need to explain what flaying is, because all of you own my previous book. If not, I'll wait while you go buy it (or borrow it from your local library). Back? OK, so you now know that to flay something is to remove its skin. This technique adds the finishing touch to many pumpkins—both ugly and intricate—and looks especially cool on squashes, most of which have a creepy, veiny surface under their skin.

- **A ROUTER IS A MESSY TOOL,** *and the goop can really fly. Wear safety goggles if you don't want a seed in your eye.*

- **BECAUSE A ROUTER SPINS,** *it tends to dance around a bit. Use both hands to keep it steady, and work slowly.*

- **TO ACHIEVE A COOL LIGHTING EFFECT,** *remove only the outermost skin of the pumpkin. When you insert a high-powered light into the pumpkin, it will create a warm but eerie glow through the flayed flesh.*

THE ANGLE GRINDER
My Choice for Rearranging a Pumpkin's Face

I was first introduced to the angle grinder when I took a class in metal sculpture. There, I learned that sculptors start with a lumpy chunk of metal and use this tool to refine their design. After I used mine to grind all sorts of welds and hunks of metal, I realized that if it worked on metal, it would probably work pretty great on a pumpkin.

Guess what? I was right—the angle grinder is perfect for pumpkin sculptors, too. The angle grinder will allow you to more easily carve shapes and contours in the flesh (see the Alien Invader on page 40). Not only that, it's super-quick: You can remove all of the skin from a pumpkin or squash in about two minutes flat. If you don't have an angle grinder, a router will meet all your flaying needs, but the angle grinder is a little quicker and more fun, and you can carve yourself a metal sculpture while you're at it.

- **THE ANGLE GRINDER WORKS IN MYSTERIOUS WAYS.** *All the tools I use are fairly dangerous, but at least you know where the pumpkin you remove ends up. The angle grinder works so quickly that instead of leaving you with a pulpy, wet residue, the carved pumpkin sort of vaporizes into thin air, floating around like some kind of pumpkin fog. Eventually, I suspect that some of it settles in your lungs, and I doubt that is good for you. You may want to wear a face mask when you angle grind.*

THE DREMEL ROTARY TOOL
The Device for Detail Work

Don't say you're not getting your bang for your buck, because here's the second tool that wasn't even mentioned in my first book, *Extreme Pumpkins* (now usually referred to in certain circles as *Extreme Pumpkins I*). I use a Dremel rotary tool when I want to do detail carving, like teeth. And nothing adds to a pumpkin's character more than cavities, snaggle teeth, and fangs. This precision grinder is also useful if you want to carve a logo, the image of someone's face, or other intricate designs. (See the Tiki Pumpkin on page 48 for a design that relies heavily on the Dremel.) Until I can find a used dental drill on eBay, the Dremel tool is my choice for unlicensed pumpkin dentistry.

- **YOU CAN USE A DREMEL ROTARY TOOL** *to remove just the outer flesh of the pumpkin, or to remove big chunks of the pumpkin as well. The only drawback is that, even spinning at 15,000 revolutions per minute, the Dremel tool is a fairly slow worker.*

- **A DREMEL TOOL** *uses small rotating cutters. I usually use one with a square bit (attachment #115, if you're really interested), but you can try U-grooves and V-grooves. Experiment with the angle of the tool to figure out how to achieve the look you want.*

THE STEAK KNIFE
Detail Work the Old-Fashioned Way

Let's face it, when you need to scrape the sides of the pumpkin cavity or dig out your jack-o'-lantern's eyeball, you need something more delicate than a jigsaw. That's where your average steak knife (or boning knife) comes into play. It's thin and flexible enough to slide into any pumpkin orifice, and serrated edges are great for extracting small chunks of pumpkin flesh.

- **WHEN TWO INCISIONS** *in your pumpkin don't meet up perfectly, or you cut a wonky circle/square/triangle, use a steak knife to tidy them up.*

- **THE STEAK KNIFE** *will also come in handy when you're slicing up other vegetables for my pumpkin designs. If it's part of the set you got as a wedding present, return it to the kitchen when you're done.*

THE BIG SPOON
Low-Tech Goop-Removal Gadget

Pumpkins are full of goop. And I've found no better goop-removal tool than a simple spoon—the bigger the better. I prefer one of those large spoons that the lunch lady used to use to dole out pasta, but an ice cream scoop is a good choice too.

- **EXTREME PUMPKINS** *are not about being nice and tidy. It's okay if you leave a stringy pumpkin booger hanging from a nostril, or don't remove every last seed. You just need to remove enough of the guts to make room for the all-important light you'll be putting in the empty shell of your pumpkin.*

- **DON'T AUTOMATICALLY THROW AWAY** *the pumpkin guts. Often they are the key to a design (see the Full-Diaper Pumpkin on page 76).*

Beware: **CHAIN SAWS AND PUMPKIN CARVING DON'T MIX.** If you own a chain saw, you know that these tools are so amazingly cool you find yourself trying to come up with new ways to use them. That's why, when I wanted to make a round pumpkin into a cube, I turned to my chain saw to do the job. Though it was fun, it was overkill for certain: The chainsaw created a rooster tail of pumpkin guts that would have made a powerboat jealous. (The wall of my garage still has a streak of orange on it.) So, when it comes to pumpkin carving, I'd suggest skipping the chain saw. A hand saw works just as well for heavy-duty cuts and is almost as fast. In this case, extra horsepower is your enemy.

THE STANDARD TOOLBOX
ALTERNATIVES TO POWER TOOLS

You don't have to use power tools to create the twenty extreme pumpkins in this book. You can achieve awe-inspiring results with hand tools, too. This is what you'll need in your manual toolkit.

- **PUMPKIN-CARVING TOOLS (for smooth cuts and irregular curves):** Instead of a jigsaw, use the knife from a standard pumpkin-carving kit to carve your pumpkin's face. For more detailed work, try an X-Acto knife. These tools aren't as fast or versatile as a jigsaw, but you'll still get wicked results.

- **DRYWALL SAW (for deep cuts and tough flesh):** Instead of a reciprocating saw, use a drywall saw to carve super-sized pumpkins. This short, stiff-bladed saw is easy to find at any hardware store or home center.

- **HAND SAW (for chop jobs):** When you need to slice a pumpkin in half or chop the top off, a hand saw is perfect for the job. If you try to use a carving knife for this kind of hard-core work, you'll have a tough time.

- **CARVING CHISEL (for flaying):** Instead of a router or angle grinder, pick up a carving chisel at your neighborhood hardware store. The sharp metal blade of this little hand tool is good for flaying the skin off your pumpkin, whether you want to remove small patches or the entire thing. If you're working with a squash, a vegetable peeler will usually do the trick.

EXTREME CARVING KNOW-HOW

So you've bought this book, you've bragged to all your friends that you're going to have the coolest pumpkins this year . . . now what? The old me would have told you to just wing it, but after I forgot the wrench I needed to change saw blades during my first TV appearance, I figured it was time for a plan.

SNACKS AND TUNES

You'll need to keep yourself going during your carving venture. I suggest candy. 'Tis the season! And you've got to have tunes when carving pumpkins. Punk rock!

POWER WASHING YOUR PUMPKINS

I like to buy pumpkins straight from the patch, but in a pinch I'll get them anywhere, any way. Regardless of where you buy them, pumpkins need a good cleaning. I like to hose down a bunch of them at once, with a pressure washer. If you don't own a pressure washer, simply stop at a coin-op car wash on your way home and pop in a few quarters.

WHAT NOT TO WEAR

Avoid loose-fitting clothing when working with power tools. I'm not trying to get you to flaunt your bulges; loose clothing could get sucked into the power tools, with you and your bulges soon to follow. Be warned: You will almost certainly get pumpkin guts all over everything you're wearing.

GOOP-PROOFING YOUR WORK AREA

I carve my pumpkins on a work bench, but any table will do. To save your space from pumpkin guts, use plastic tablecloths and a plastic drop cloth for the floor—they're miles better than newspapers, which just turn into a soggy mess. Some power tools (like the angle grinder) will cause pumpkin spray to go everywhere. For the messy tools, your best bet is to work out-of-doors.

THE CARE AND FEEDING OF POWER TOOLS

Get all of your tools together before you start, because midway through your carving session you'll be a gutsy mess, and in no shape to rummage though your house looking for your electric drill. Before you begin, make sure all batteries are charged and all blades are straight. After you're through, unplug the tools or remove their batteries, and clean them as best you can. Let them sit for a day or two, then blow out any dried residue with compressed air. Don't expect perfection: Anyone who looked at my tools would know that I carve pumpkins with them, thanks to the significant layer of dried pumpkin guts on them.

EXTREME CLEAN-UP

When carving pumpkins, you'll need to clean as you go. Otherwise, your hands and the pumpkin will get slippery. I find that the absorbent surface of old towels works best for mopping up pumpkin juices. Towels also have the added benefit of traction—if your pumpkin refuses to sit still while you're carving it, put the towel underneath it to keep it steady. When you're done carving, wipe up any remaining pumpkin guts and follow it up with a cleaning spray that includes bleach. (That seems to keep away the mold and critters.) Pumpkin guts are heavy: Use a cardboard box lined with a trash bag as a receptacle. That way, you can just tape the box shut and take it to the curb.

SUPER-COOL WAYS TO LIGHT UP YOUR PUMPKIN

When it comes time to light your Extreme Pumpkin, here are five awesome methods to make it glow.

- **Kerosene: For Killer Flames and Dark, Stinky Smoke.** As a Boy Scout I learned that a toilet paper roll soaked in kerosene will create flames three feet high. This ultra-impressive bonfire lasts for a glorious forty-five minutes or so. Kerosene is available at almost every hardware story, so go get some.

- **Charcoal Lighter Fluid: For Less Smokey Flames.** For a little less smoke, use charcoal lighter fluid. Soaking a roll of toilet paper with the stuff is good, but so is filling the pumpkin with crinkled-up newspaper and lighting that. The newspaper won't burn as long, but it does engulf the entire inside of the pumpkin with flame. And that makes for a great photo-op.

> **Beware:** Don't light up a jack-o'-lantern inside your home—or without adult supervision. Satanic flames belong in an open outdoor area, far away from anything flammable. Always keep a fire extinguisher handy and know how to use it. And, remember, anything hot can burn you. Fire is hot, so are tiki torches and spotlights. Steer clear.

- **Glow Sticks: For a Creepy Glow.** When I carve an Alien Intruder squash (see page 40), I feel strongly that it should emit a strange green glow. To do this, snap a bunch of glow sticks so that they start glowing, then use a pair of heavy-duty scissors or garden shears to open them. Most glow sticks are nontoxic, but check the label before you snip. Insert the glow sticks in your jack-'o-lantern and stand back to watch the fallout.

- **Spotlight: For Good Aim.** Spotlights are perfect for the inside of a jack-o'-lantern because they aim their light in one direction. Spotlights are also nice for illuminating pumpkins that can't be lit from the inside because of their design. But my favorite thing about spotlights is that they come cheap at your neighborhood home center. Because who wants to spend $40 on a light fixture for the inside of a pumpkin?

- **Tiki Torch: For a Laid-Back Vibe.** Lighting pumpkins using some kind of vessel of fuel with a wick in it sounds pretty cool. Fortunately, you can do just that with a tiki torch, which you can buy at home or discount stores, especially during the summer. Get a tiki torch with a removable pole, take off the top, and put it inside your pumpkin. If necessary, fill it with whatever kind of fuel the manufacturer recommends. Light it, sit back, and enjoy the nice flame for hours. It looks especially great with a Tiki Pumpkin (see page 48)!

PROBLEM CHILD
PUMPKIN

WHEN IT COMES TO MANAGING KIDS, THERE ARE TWO TYPES OF PEOPLE IN THIS WORLD:
Kid-Wranglers and Greenhorns. Kid-Wranglers have experience with kids, and have learned the tricks and traps necessary to get them to do whatever needs to be done. Greenies, on the other hand, are a little frightened by children, and they try to use reason and logic on them. Those Greenies are so silly. Like a drunk who wanders onto the field of a sporting event, their futile efforts keep us all entertained. Here's how to make a Problem Child Pumpkin guaranteed to make all the Greenies in your neighborhood squirm.

YOU'LL NEED

- 1 tall pumpkin

- CARVING AND GUTTING TOOLS: jigsaw, steak knife, saw, big metal spoon

  NOTE: Power tools are optional. *(See The Standard Toolbox: Alternatives to Power Tools, page 9.)*

- Dry erase marker

- Clothes for your Problem Child: a pair of old gloves, kids' shoes, kids' pants

- Scissors

- Drill

- 8 to 12 screws *(any kind will do—it's just a pumpkin!)*

- 3 pieces of 1 x 1-inch or 2 x 2-inch scrap wood *that are 14 to 24 inches (35 to 60 cm) long*

- Old newspaper

- Glue *of some kind (I use a hot-melt glue gun)*

- A pumpkin-carving knife *or some other comical weapon, real or otherwise (see Beware box, opposite)*

Jack-o'- Lantern Juvenile Delinquent

1. **CUT** open and **GUT** your pumpkin from the top.

2. **DRAW** and then **CARVE** an angry-kid face into the pumpkin. When drawing the mouth, consider leaving some gaps between the teeth.

3. Have your pumpkin try on the pants, and if they are too small for the base of your pumpkin, use the scissors to **CUT** a slit in the back of the waistband, so that the opening is large enough. If they are too large, just keep **FOLDING** over the waistband until the pants are snug around the pumpkin.

4. Attach the newly fitted pants to the base of your jack-o'-lantern by **DRILLING** the screws through the waistband and into the pumpkin. Put the first screw in front and center, then proceed around the pumpkin from both the right and the left, working your way to the back. This way, any excess material will end up hidden at the back of the pumpkin.

5 **CUT** two of the pieces of wood to the same length, about 4 inches (10 cm) longer than you want the legs to be. With a saw, **SHARPEN** one end of each piece of wood, then put them into the pant legs and **SHOVE** the sharp ends into the pumpkin.

6 **CUT** the third piece of wood a couple of inches (5 cm) shorter than the other leg pieces. **SHARPEN** it on one end as well. Use this piece of wood to prop up your Problem Child Pumpkin by **CUTTING** a hole in the butt area of the pants and inserting the sharp end of the piece of wood through it and into your pumpkin. Because this piece of wood is slightly shorter, your pumpkin should lean back a bit.

7 **STUFF** the gloves with newspaper to make them look like hands. **GLUE** the comical weapon to the glove, or use more than one item and glue them to both gloves.

8 Attach the gloves to either side of the pumpkin by **DRILLING** two screws through the base of the wrist of each glove and into the pumpkin.

9 Put the shoes on the ground and **PLACE** the wooden "legs" in them. **BE GRATEFUL** this Problem Child is only a pumpkin.

Beware: Children and sharp objects don't mix. If kids are going to mingle with this Problem Child, substitute plastic toy weapons for the pumpkin-carving tool shown in photo.

EXTREME PARENTING

HOW TO DEAL WITH HALLOWEEN CANDY-INDUCED TANTRUMS

We've all seen it: too much candy leading to kids throwing fits, resisting bedtime, and climbing onto the roof and refusing to come down. Here are some suggestions for coping when your offspring are high on sugar.

1) Unless your kid is really out of control (kicking, screaming bloody murder), try ignoring her. A martini or two usually helps.

2) If ignoring your kid is futile, make funny faces or crazy noises, do a funny dance, or pretend to fall. If he is still screaming for more candy, do not get up.

3) Alternatively, let him know how you feel: "I feel like handing you over to your mom," "I feel like telling Santa Claus about how naughty you are," or "I feel like a drink."

4) No matter what, don't give in to your child's cries for more candy. Remember, you'll need something to eat after he finally goes to bed.

5) If all else fails, give her a Bit-O-Honey. These candies take a long time to eat, so you'll get a little break. (Be sure to save the mini candy bars for yourself.)

ANGRY MOB PUMPKIN

THIS DESIGN ISN'T JUST A FUN LAWN DECORATION, it is a declaration. An anti-establishment sign that extreme pumpkin carvers can use to proclaim: "We're here, and very rude, get used to us. We're tired of cutesy porch flags featuring friendly ghosts and cupcakes wearing witches' hats. Instead, we're carving up as many big, bad, truly tasteless pumpkins as our power tools can churn out." This Halloween there will be millions of little pumpkins eating big pumpkins on porches across the country. If you see a mysterious unmarked car driving by your house don't be concerned—it's just the Halloween establishment, getting nervous.

Squash Authority!

YOU'LL NEED

- **1 very large pumpkin**

- **CARVING AND GUTTING TOOLS:** reciprocating saw, jigsaw, steak knife, big metal spoon

  NOTE: Power tools are optional. *(See The Standard Toolbox: Alternatives to Power Tools, page 9.)*

- **Dry erase marker**

- **4 to 8 smaller pumpkins** *(no more than one-quarter the height of the large pumpkin)*

- **Several screws, nails, dowels, or pieces of wire** *(for attaching the little pumpkins to the big pumpkin)*

- **An "overthrow the establishment" sort of mentality,** *along with a forged passport just in case you need to leave the country in a hurry*

BEGIN WITH LARGE PUMPKIN

1. **CUT** off part of the top of your pumpkin, but go for realism. If little pumpkins were eating this pumpkin alive, they wouldn't eat a perfect circle at its top.

2. **GUT** your pumpkin, but reserve some of the guts for step 5.

3. **DRAW** and then **CARVE** an agonizing face on the large pumpkin. This fat-cat has seen his last days at the top of the food chain. Showcase his fall from grace with a gruesome expression.

4. **CUT** two or three holes in the top and sides of the pumpkin, big enough to place the smaller pumpkins inside them.

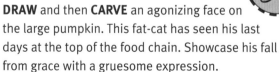

5. **PLACE** some of the guts in front of the pumpkin, with some coming out of his mouth.

CONTINUE WITH SMALL PUMPKINS

6. **GUT** and **CARVE** some of the smallest pumpkins. **PLACE** these pumpkins in front of the pumpkin by the guts. These pumpkins may lack the courage it takes to bite first, but once the establishment starts to fall, all sorts will gather round to feed off its carcass.

7. **GUT** and **CARVE** some pumpkins with only top teeth. **REMOVE** their lower jaws and attach them to the top of the pumpkin with the screws, nails, dowels, or pieces of wire. This mob scene is getting ugly.

8. **GUT** and **CARVE** the rest of your menacing small pumpkins. **SLICE** off the bottom one-third of each, then install them in the holes you made in step 4. This will make it look like the smaller pumpkins are burrowing into the skull of the large pumpkin. Use the screws, nails, dowels, or wire to help attach them to the big pumpkin, if necessary.

9. **DISPLAY** your pride by putting this big-ass pumpkin right on your front porch. Direct its intimidating glare toward your co-op board, your employer, or even your state capital; just make sure that everyone can see it.

EXTREME HALLOWEEN

SIX THINGS TO LOOK FORWARD TO WHEN PUMPKIN CARVERS TAKE OVER THE WORLD

1) October 31 will be a half-day of work.

2) Houses that don't give away Halloween candy will be ticketed.

3) Tennis courts nationwide will be turned into pumpkin-carving areas. (Special orange dumpsters will be brought in for the guts.)

4) Kids' costumes will come with a hook on the back, and it will be socially acceptable to attach one of those retractable dog leashes to it before you take your child trick-or-treating.

5) High school students will learn pumpkin carving in shop class, and *Extreme Pumpkins I* and *II* will be required reading. School nurses will be certified to reattach severed fingers.

6) Power tools, fake blood, and other essential pumpkin-carving supplies will be sold tax free, while adorable Halloween items will be taxed as heavily as cigarettes and booze.

BARBECUED PUMPKIN

I LIKE FOOD AND I LIKE FIRE. Combine the two, throw in a pumpkin, and here you are: the Barbecued Pumpkin. This extreme pumpkin isn't a jack-o'-lantern you leave on your front stoop—it's a party gimmick that will teach your guests the true meaning of Halloween. Why not invite the neighbors over for a barbecue, and reaffirm their belief that living near someone like you is bringing down their property values? Just be sure to have a camera ready—and a fire extinguisher too.

Give Your Pumpkin the Third Degree

YOU'LL NEED

- **1 pumpkin** *(any size)*

- **CARVING AND GUTTING TOOLS:**
  jigsaw, steak knife, big metal
  spoon

  NOTE: Power tools are optional.
  (See The Standard Toolbox:
  Alternatives to Power Tools,
  page 9.)

- **Dry erase marker**

- **A grill**

- **Lighter fluid** *(optional, but fun)*

- **Fire extinguisher**

1. **CUT** a round plug in the bottom or top of your pumpkin and **REMOVE** the guts.

2. **DRAW** and then **CARVE** a silly, pained expression on the face of your jack-o'-lantern. The pumpkin will collapse downward as it roasts. To give the face an under-bite as it collapses, angle the saw from above as you carve the mouth.

3. Put the pumpkin on the grill.

4. **DOUSE** the pumpkin (and the charcoal under the grate if you have a charcoal grill) with lighter fluid.

Beware: Hey, you! Yeah, you, the person who's about to light a pumpkin on fire. You have a fire extinguisher handy, right? And I take it that you're outdoors, away from anything flammable? I hope that you kept the hairspray to a minimum today, because burning your own hair off is just embarrassing. Anyway, bud, don't forget that a great pumpkin is worth the effort, but it isn't worth lighting yourself, anyone else, or any of your hard-earned stuff on fire. Pay attention, don't leave the fire unattended, and take it easy with the lighter fluid.

5) **LIGHT** it up!

6) **TAKE** some photos. Your pumpkin will start to get mushy in about an hour. Why not leave it on the grill to surprise someone?

PUMPKIN PRANKS

SIX PLACES TO LEAVE A BARBECUED PUMPKIN

After you've frightened trick-or-treaters with your ingenious charred jack-o'-lantern, don't just toss out your creation. Take it one step further by scaring the stuffing out of your friends and loved ones! Here is a helpful list of some good places to leave a dead pumpkin.

1) In the fridge, preferably presented on a nice antique platter.

2) In your kid's closet—because children let loose the shrillest screams.

3) À la *The Godfather*: on someone's pillow.

4) Bobbing in the bathtub, or, if it fits, the toilet bowl.

5) The backseat of your wife's car—capitalize on that creepy "Is there someone in here with me?" feeling.

6) In a dark corner of the basement or garage—if they don't see it, they will eventually smell it!

SKELLINGTON PUMPKIN

THE NIGHTMARE BEFORE CHRISTMAS IS A MUST-SEE MOVIE. Not only is it a masterpiece of animation directed by one of the weirdest filmmakers in cinema (Tim Burton), it is the ultimate Halloween-versus-Christmas film. If you've seen it, you'll recognize our next pumpkin character. It's Jack Skellington, the pumpkin king of Halloween Town. After you construct your homage to this ever-important figure in Halloween lore, invite the uninitiated over and have a movie screening. With a fantastic yard decoration like Jack Skellington, you'll never get sick of Halloween festivities.

Boys and Girls of Every Age, Don't You Want to See Something Strange?

YOU'LL NEED

- **1 white pumpkin that's larger than a human head** *(readily available in most pumpkin patches)*

- **Dry erase marker**

- **CARVING TOOL: jigsaw**

  NOTE: Power tools are optional. *(See The Standard Toolbox: Alternatives to Power Tools, page 9.)*

- **1 life-sized plastic skeleton**

1. Take the lazy approach to Jack's head, and don't gut it. I like to leave this one with the guts inside to give his eyes and mouth a strange and stringy appearance. You will probably want to **DRAW** Jack's face on before you start cutting.

2. **CARVE** the eyes. Jack's eyes are roughly the shape of two eggs leaning in toward one another. He's not quite handsome, so a lack of symmetry is fine.

3. **SLICE** out a couple of nostrils, too. The top part of the nostrils should be just level with the bottom of the eyes. The nostrils are also egg-shaped, but much smaller—only about one-fifth the size of Jack's eyes.

4. **CARVE** the mouth. Jack has a wide, narrow grin, with notches between his teeth. He has many teeth that are only roughly the same size, and his outer teeth are not as square as the ones in the center.

5) If your plastic skeleton is like mine, the skull will pop right off. **TAKE** it off, and save it for another project (see sidebar).

6) **CUT** a hole in the bottom of the pumpkin and insert the top of the skeleton's spine into it.

7) **LEAVE** Mr. Skellington in the yard where everyone can say hello.

SKULLDUGGERY

FIVE DEVIOUS THINGS TO DO WITH A SKELETON'S HEAD

After you've carved a pumpkin head for your skeleton, you'll have an extra skull. And, let me tell you, having a spare skull around is a strange feeling. It shouldn't take long before you find a use for it. (Who can stand that vacant stare?) But in case you're having trouble, here is what I ended up doing with mine.

1) The first thing I did was practice my Shakespeare: "Alas, Poor Yorick! I knew him, Horatio, a fellow of infinite jest, of most excellent fancy. . . ." That didn't last long, because I only knew the passage through the word "Yorick." I had to look the rest up.

2) Next, I placed the skull on the dashboard of my minivan. Tacky, you say? I'll try anything for a little inspiration. Besides, I figured that if just one scared motorist got out of my way it would be worth it.

3) Of course, I couldn't resist sticking the skull in my fridge. My wife is used to my antics, so I got only a lukewarm reaction, but you might really frighten someone.

4) Another great thing to do with a skull: Freak out the people who run your local haunted house. No one cares when you walk into a haunted house holding a skull, but when you walk out, everyone will swear you're stealing it. That's when I start running, just to cause some drama.

5) Now I just use the skull to impress the ladies. Chicks dig a guy with a plastic skull.

FOUL PLAY
PUMPKIN

OU⟨H! Your beloved baseball team just crashed and burned in the postseason. What are you going to do? Express your disappointment in a pumpkin carving, of course. Doesn't everyone do that? Maybe I'm the only one. But no matter what your personal outlet is, here is a fun carving for the baseball fan: the Foul Play Pumpkin (sorry, couldn't resist the pun). After all, at the end of October, most of us have plenty of time for Halloween crafts, since our team has let us down (again) long before then.

Sitting in a Cheap Seat? Better Pay Attention!

YOU'LL NEED:

- **1 pumpkin** *(choose one slightly larger than a human head)*

- **CARVING AND GUTTING TOOLS:** jigsaw, steak knife, big metal spoon

  NOTE: Power tools are optional. *(See The Standard Toolbox: Alternatives to Power Tools, page 9.)*

- **Dry erase marker**

- **A baseball**

- **Glue** *(white glue works fine)*

1. **CUT** open and **GUT** your pumpkin. You can do it from the top or the bottom; it doesn't matter to me. Be your own boss! **SAVE** 4 to 6 seeds and **DRY** them immediately with a paper towel. Leave them someplace warm and dry for the time being.

2. **DRAW** and then **CARVE** the nose and mouth, and one eye that is pinched closed like it is crying.

3. For the second eye (the "baseball" eye), **CARVE** a tapered hole that is a bit smaller than the baseball. By "tapered," I mean the hole should get smaller as you work your way into the pumpkin. The largest part of the hole should still be smaller than the baseball.

4. **FIT** your baseball into the eye. You want it to fit snugly, so that when you push the ball into the pumpkin it's gripped by the pumpkin flesh. If the

hole is too small (as it should be), **SHAVE** away the pumpkin skin around it little by little until you get it just right. If the hole is too big, go find a softball (ha, ha). If it's too big for a softball, go find a basketball and paint it white, and then go see an optometrist.

5) **DRY** the outside of your pumpkin with a paper towel, then **GLUE** the pumpkin seeds to the face of the pumpkin. They should look like tears.

6) **PLACE** the pumpkin someplace where other fans of your team can share in your disappointment.

PUMPKIN PRANK
PUMPKIN FULL OF PENNIES

I love playing tricks on kids because a) everything is new to them, and so b) they almost always fall for them. Pumpkins and pumpkin patches are typically a big mystery to kids. Unless they live on a farm, the idea that dirt, water, and sunlight can produce a large, orange globe is quite strange. It is no surprise, then, to find a child who has absolutely no idea what's inside a pumpkin. That is why I fill pumpkins with pennies whenever a six- to eight-year-old comes over for a pumpkin-carving party. Here's how:

1) **CUT** a slit, no larger than the side of a penny, in a divot, crease, or somewhere else on the pumpkin where it won't be too obvious.

2) Start **INSERTING** pennies into the slot, using one to push the next all the way into the cavity of the pumpkin. Watch some TV, relax, bake a cake, whatever you want to do, just keep putting those coins into the pumpkin. Force the last penny in using the blade of your knife or saw.

3) **HIDE** the slot using some dirt, grass, or pumpkin guts.

4) **GIVE** the pumpkin to an unsuspecting child. **PRETEND** nothing unusual is happening when he carves the pumpkin, releasing a jackpot of coins.

SUBLIMINAL MESSAGE PUMPKIN

WE'VE ALL HEARD STORIES ABOUT SUBLIMINAL ADVERTISING—hidden messages functioning below the threshold of our consciousness to make us **buy** stuff we don't need. What's surprising is that it's never been conclusively shown to work—at least, the studies I've seen seem totally bogus. Nevertheless, the idea of subliminal advertising has entered our consciousness just like other hoaxes and scams. Though subliminal messages may not work in real life, they look great on **my** pumpkins, and they are spooky since even the suggestion of mind control creeps people out. To make a Subliminal Message Pumpkin, you carve only from the back, leaving its front surface completely unblemished. Once you light it up in the dark, a message shows through. Be sure to make it as scary as the one featured in this **book.**

Drill Fear Right into Their Minds

YOU'LL NEED

- **1 pumpkin** (*a smooth-skinned one is easiest to work with*)

- **CARVING AND GUTTING TOOLS: jigsaw, steak knife, big metal spoon, Dremel tool with a square bit**

  NOTE: Power tools are optional. (*Substitute a square-tipped chisel for the Dremel tool. See also The Standard Toolbox: Alternatives to Power Tools, page 9.*)

- **A permanent marker**

- **Hard work surface** *that can take some abuse (don't do this design on the dining room table!)*

- **A bright light** (*I use a red light bulb mounted in a work light*)

(1) **CUT** a large hole—and it can be really large—in the back of your pumpkin and **REMOVE** the guts.

(2) **SCRAPE** the inside on the opposite side of front of the pumpkin, so that it is fairly smooth and even.

(3) Using your marker, **DRAW** a mirror image on this surface of the message you'd like to display. (The mirror image on the inside will read correctly from the outside.)

(4) **CARVE** wherever you have marked. The valleys you carve should be almost (but not quite) as deep as the pumpkin is thick. In other words, carve away as much of your pumpkin's yellow flesh as you can without poking through the front of the pumpkin. Here are some tips on how to accomplish this tricky feat:

Subliminal Tips

- Carve with the pumpkin face down on a hard work surface. As you get close to the skin of the pumpkin you can actually start to feel the hardness of the work surface. This will help you know when to stop.

- Check your progress as you go by shining a light from behind the pumpkin and seeing if you can see it from the front.

- Poke the pumpkin with a pin to give yourself an idea of how thick the skin that remains is. This will leave a mark, though, so only do it if you have to.

- Add pumpkin guts to the backside to plug holes or if your carving needs some adjustment.

- If you do poke through the skin, try using some waterproof wood glue to put it back together.

 5 LIGHT the pumpkin from behind with a bright light. I like using a spot light, especially when I hook it up to one of those light-flasher do-hickeys that makes the light pulse when something near it makes a loud sound.

WHAT TO WRITE?

SUBLIMINAL MESSAGES BETTER LEFT ALONE

So the real question is, what should you write on your pumpkin? You may think you've hit on a winning phrase, but my experience reveals that subliminal messages can be misinterpreted.

- **Boo!** The written word boo! has never been scary, so don't even try it. By the time your subject reads it, all of the surprise is gone. You might as well have written the word pumpkin on your pumpkin.

- **loo8.** This is what I told people my pumpkin spelled when I accidentally carved "boo!" the correct way, which made it read backward from the front (don't try carving while watching the game). People started flocking to the house across the street, whose number was 1008.

- **Go away.** Unless "Go away" is now slang for "Take all of my candy," people don't seem to take this Subliminal Message Pumpkin very seriously.

- **Fear.** A little fear is usually a good thing, until people stop going to your website or buying your book. I need to send my kids to college somehow.

- **Kill.** Let's just say, this one won't be appreciated by the block committee.

SNOT-SHOOTER PUMPKIN

SNEEZING IS PERFECT SUBJECT MATTER FOR A JACK-O'-LANTERN because sneezing is gross. All that effluvia exiting the body in a violent manner—yuck. Sneezing is also funny. Not necessarily immediately "ha ha" funny, but funny more in the manner of "I can't believe the booger that was hanging out of Craig Melanson's nose at recess." And *booger* is such a fun word to say. BOOGER! See, I said it, and it was funny. Booger! I got you again. I dare you to approach me at a book signing and say, "Booger!" I guarantee we will both smile.

Blast Some Boogers!

YOU'LL NEED

- **1 pumpkin** (*any size or shape should do—everyone sneezes*)

- **CARVING AND GUTTING TOOLS: jigsaw, steak knife, big metal spoon**

  NOTE: Power tools are optional. (*See The Standard Toolbox: Alternatives to Power Tools, page 9.*)

- **Piece of wire** (*the thickness of a coat hanger or thinner*)

- **Wire cutters**

1. **GUT** your pumpkin. You can **CUT** off the bottom or the top; it's your choice. **RESERVE** the goop and seeds.

2. **CARVE** a sneezy face on your pumpkin. Squinty eyes and flared nostrils are hallmarks of a sneezy face. The mouth should be closed and shown as just a line.

3. **CUT** a length of wire that reaches from the nostril of the pumpkin to the ground at a diagonal. **BEND** it 90 degrees at one end.

PLUNGE the bent end into the flesh of the pumpkin's nostril. (Can you imagine how much having a length of wire jabbed into the flesh inside your nose would hurt? I plucked a nose hair once and it made my eyes water.)

 THREAD some pumpkin guts and chunks onto the wire. Think of it as a big snot kabob. Yum!

6. To gross out the maximum number of neighbors, **GIVE** this pumpkin pride of place in your front yard.

Beware: If you think boogers are funny (and you know you do), then your kids and their snotty little friends are sure to find them HILARIOUS. In fact, the sight of a Snot-Shooter Pumpkin is likely to incite endless snickering, annoying chants of "Booger, booger, booger," and possibly voluble nose blowing (or rude pantomimes of such). I herewith decline all responsibility.

EXTREME VARIATION
PROJECTILE VOMITING PUMPKIN

If sneezing is gross, puking is definitely grosser. In my first book, *Extreme Pumpkins,* I created a puking pumpkin, but I hear dribbling puke is so last Halloween season. If you want to be au courant you will need to make that puke appear to fly. Here is how to make a projectile vomiting pumpkin that'll make even the least squeamish among us want to retch.

1) **GUT** the pumpkin as you did with the Snot-Shooter Pumpkin. If you want lots of puke, you may require the guts of a couple of pumpkins.

2) **CARVE** the pumpkin just like the Snot-Shooter Pumpkin, but with a gaping mouth.

3) **THREAD** the guts of the pumpkin on several lengths of wire (ten to fifteen should do it). You should have guts streaming from the mouth, nose, perhaps even dribbling out of the ears. In other words, there should be guts exiting everywhere except the eyeballs. The eyes are left plain to show misery.

ALIEN INVADER

WITCHES, GHOSTS, AND JACK-O'-LANTERNS USED TO BE THE ONLY HALLOWEEN SPOOKS AROUND.

Later, werewolves, vampires, and mummies entered the game. Now, the holiday is celebrated with all sorts of tertiary creatures. You have your Jasons, your Freddy Kruegers, Chuckie dolls, members of the Munsters and Addams families . . . and then there are the aliens. How did aliens get attached to Halloween? Using the same logic that has polar bears and penguins hanging around at Christmas, I've deduced that it's because aliens don't have a holiday to call their own. So I thought I'd honor them with their own design, and since October 31 has become a bit of a free-for-all, I've let some squashes in on the fun.

Close Encounters of the Squash Kind

YOU'LL NEED

- **1 green winter squash** (the one I used is called a "greenstripey" [by me] or a "green-striped cushaw" [by everyone else])

- **An unrepressed memory** of an alien who woke you up one night to tractor-beam you into his spaceship for scientific tests

- **Dry erase marker**

- **CARVING TOOLS: jigsaw, steak knife, angle grinder or Dremel tool**

  NOTE: Power tools are optional. (See The Standard Toolbox: Alternatives to Power Tools, page 9.)

- **Glow sticks or a spotlight with a green lightbulb** (optional)

1. Using your unrepressed memory (or this picture) as a reference, **DRAW** a face on your strangely alien head–shaped squash. **DRAW** an iris inside each eye.

2. Begin **CARVING** the eyes, starting at the irises and **GRINDING** away the skin as you work toward the outer edges of the eyes, leaving more flesh closer to the irises to make them appear as though they are bulging out of the skull. If you're not lucky enough to have an angle grinder, **CUT** slits to the outer shape of the eyes, cutting deeper into the squash as you get closer to the outer edges, where you should be about ¼ inch (.6 cm) in. Then **SLICE** outward to remove the chunks of the skin.

3. **GOUGE** out the irises, then follow along the outer edges with your tool to smooth and round out the eyes.

4. **CARVE** out the mouth and nose (in this case, nostrils).

5. If you want your Alien to have a creepier texture, **SHAVE** all of the skin off of your greenstripey.

6) **ACTIVATING** a pair of glow sticks and stuffing them in the Alien's eye sockets is fun, but not quite eerie enough for me. To illuminate the whole head, **CARVE** a hole in the back and **SCOOP** out the pulp.

7) **INSERT** the glow sticks or spotlight with a green lightbulb inside the Alien's head. Alien-a-rific!

PUMPKIN PRANK

THE ALLIGATOR HEAD

Designing with squashes is great because they often already look like what you're trying to make. A greenstripey already looks a lot like an alien head, and many Hubbard squashes already look like alligator heads. All you have to do is put the teeth and eyes on it and put it somewhere startling—like coming out of a storm drain.

1) DRAW an eye and teeth on one side of the squash with a dry erase marker. Do one side at a time, so that if you mess it up, you'll have a "do-over" on the other side.

2) CARVE the eyes just like you did with the alien head, but this time shave away more skin from around the irises, so they look like they are sunken into the head.

3) CARVE the teeth. Realistic alligator teeth overlap the opposite lip—in other words, the bottom teeth should extend upward past the top of the upper teeth. Alligator teeth look random, so try to avoid a pattern. Also, their mouths aren't a straight line, but are more like a meandering boundary of death.

4) POSE the Alligator Head someplace cool, like sticking out of the storm drain. Or use it to peek out of an alligator-shaped pile of leaves.

AFRAID OF PIE PUMPKIN

IF YOU WERE A PUMPKIN, I IMAGINE YOUR BIGGEST FEAR would be getting turned into a pumpkin pie. After all, what could be worse than being plucked from the pumpkin patch and sent to a pie-filling manufacturer, where your identity would be stripped away as you were slowly roasted, pureed, and scattered among a bunch of different cans? Eventually, you'd be made into a cracked and overseasoned pie. Your casket spray would include whipped cream, and the pallbearers would each be holding a fork. Want to show your sympathy for this ultimate pumpkin death sentence? Carve up this postmortem protest pumpkin.

The Only Fate WORSE than CARVING

YOU'LL NEED

- **1 pumpkin** *(one that is slightly larger than a human head is a great choice)*

- **CARVING AND GUTTING TOOLS: jigsaw, steak knife, big metal spoon**

  NOTE: Power tools are optional. *(See The Standard Toolbox: Alternatives to Power Tools, page 9.)*

- **Dry erase marker**

- **1 pie crust in tin**

- **Other pumpkin pie ingredients, such as sugar, eggs, vanilla extract, sweetened condensed milk, nutmeg, cinnamon, and don't forget the whipped cream** *(Since most people don't actually know what's in pumpkin pie, you need only a few ingredients to get the idea across.)*

- **Glow sticks or spotlight**

(1) **CUT** open and **GUT** your pumpkin.

(2) **DRAW** a frightened face on the pumpkin. When pumpkins get scared, their eyes get big and their mouth opens in a funny shape (with the ends turned downward). **CARVE** the face with the eyes looking down and to the side, where your pie ingredients will be.

(3) **PLACE** all of the ingredients in the pie crust and **POSITON** it in the line of sight of the poor pumpkin.

(4) **ILLUMINATE** the pumpkin using glow sticks or a spotlight.

(5) **HAVE** a good chuckle at what you've just created. That pumpkin sure looks scared!

WHAT DO CARVING PUMPKINS TASTE LIKE?

A TASTE TEST FOR LOVERS OF ALL THINGS PUMPKIN

Although I feel for those terrified pumpkins facing death by pie, I have to admit that I love a good pumpkin pie—not to mention pumpkin ravioli, pumpkin bread, and other pumpkin-flavored items. Since my family typically makes these items with canned pumpkin, I wondered if I would like the taste of a traditional carving pumpkin. I decided to perform a taste test.

I tried roasting three different pumpkins for comparison's sake: a small "pie pumpkin," a fancy pumpkin squash called a "Musquée de Provence," and a fairly large carved "jack-o'-lantern" pumpkin. Here's what I found:

- **THE SMALL "PIE PUMPKIN":** This pumpkin was easy to roast. Sliced, it tasted like a sweet winter squash. I can see why it's known as "pie pumpkin"—I'd be happy to see this pumpkin end up in my pie.

- **THE "MUSQUÉE DE PROVENCE":** This is a dark orange winter squash that looks like a garden-variety pumpkin, except flatter with deep vertical grooves. My pumpkin farmer friend told me that in France, fairly pricey slices of these squashes are sold by the pound. (Luckily, I didn't have to pay a premium—at the pumpkin patch all squashes are the same price.) The pie pumpkin was good, but the Musquée de Provence was really good. The roasted slices tasted similar to butternut squash, but they had a denser, sweeter flavor. Although I'm sure it would make a delicious pie, why go to the trouble? I'd eat these slices right out of the oven.

- **THE LARGE "JACK-O'-LANTERN" PUMPKIN:** Last of all, I tasted the jack-o-lantern, which was amazing—amazingly bland, that is. Years of cultivating for size have eliminated all the flavor from this carved pumpkin squash—which was little more than a watery shell. Yuck. I tried roasting it further to see if I could concentrate the flavors (that's what they seem to recommend on cooking shows), but then it tasted like watery scorched yuck.

Conclusion: If you want to prepare a good pumpkin pie, go with a small, dense pie pumpkin. If you want to make roasted pumpkin or another savory dish, don't be afraid to try an exotic squash, like the Musquée de Provence. (Try mashing it up like my mom used to—with plenty of butter, salt, and pepper. Yum!) But I can't recommend that you reuse your jack-o'-lantern—unless you want to pay penance for his untimely demise.

TIKI PUMPKIN

I LIKE TIKI STUFF. You know, those Leilani skull mugs that you get at Polynesian restaurants or those kitschy zombie paintings you see at hot-rod shows. I even like the tchotchkes that Hawaiian artists have to create to keep the tourists happy. Their angry faces always make me smile (though this must say something unflattering about my personality). When I realized that tiki carvings and jack-o'-lanterns have a lot in common, this cool Polynesian-style pumpkin was born. A top-notch porch display, it's also perfect for lighting up a Halloween party. Pair with plenty of tropical beverages for your guests.

Pumpkin Carving's Big Kahuna

YOU'LL NEED

- **1 big, tall pumpkin**

- **CARVING AND GUTTING TOOLS:** jigsaw, big metal spoon, Dremel tool with a square bit

  NOTE: Power tools are optional. *(Substitute a square-tipped chisel for the Dremel tool. See also The Standard Toolbox: Alternatives to Power Tools, page 9.)*

- **2 differently colored dry erase markers**

- **Picture of a tiki you want to carve** *(try TikiFarm.com for some inspirational designs)*

- **A red light source or flame,** *such as a small lamp with a red or flicker-flame light bulb, a tiki torch and fuel, or an oil lamp*

- **Cool South Pacific tunes and a fruity beverage** *(optional)*

1. **GUT** your pumpkin from below. You'll be creating a real masterpiece here, so you'll want it to look as clean as possible. Hiding the giant clean-out hole is a great first step.

2. **SKETCH** your tiki design onto the pumpkin. Use one color for areas to remove completely and another color for areas where you will remove just the skin, leaving some of the flesh. Don't worry if you're not entirely sure which should be which at first. The dry erase marker will rub off and you can have another go at it.

CARVE the areas that will have some flesh remaining, using different angles and depths for different looks. Deeper carving will let more light out; shallower carving will let less light out. Going all the way through the pumpkin flesh will let everyone know you messed up. Check out page 35 for some tips on how to know if you've carved deeply enough.

 CUT out the areas that need to be removed completely.

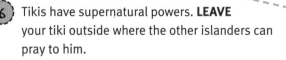

Beware: There's a reason I told you to gut your pumpkin from the bottom. This way, you can light up your tiki torch or other fire source of choice, then safely reposition your tiki pumpkin over the flame. (Lighting a pumpkin from the top is a surefire way to burn your hand. Don't do it.)

 LIGHT the pumpkin to create an other-worldly glow.

6 Tikis have supernatural powers. **LEAVE** your tiki outside where the other islanders can pray to him.

PUMPKIN PRANK

THE BLOOD-GUSHING PUMPKIN

Each year when Halloween is near, I get asked to make TV appearances. During a recent appearance, a talk show host and I were carving pumpkins when he began to wonder why his was oozing blood. Long story short, that show won't be asking me back (it's a good thing I don't want to be famous). Even if you don't know a talk show host to gross out, you should try your hand at this fun prank. Teenagers (especially ones who like violent video games) are an ideal target.

1) GET a marinade injector (if you don't have one, you can usually find them in the barbecue sauce section of the grocery store).

2) MAKE some fake blood using the ingredients listed on page 82.

3) FILL the injector with the fake blood, and inject it into the pumpkin.

4) If you, like me, have prepared your pumpkin for a TV appearance, I would suggest you not also rig up a blood-spurting fake finger. People don't seem to get the joke.

PUMPKIN SERPENT

WHETHER THEY LOVE THEM, HATE THEM, OR BOTH, snakes are a popular topic among little kids. You see, for a kid, every pile of leaves is a potential den of slithering, slinking serpents ready to attack. To make kids scream in delight at your pumpkin serpent, all you have to do is create something that remotely approximates a snake, and their imaginations will do the rest. You can make a specific type of snake (mine has a diamondback pattern) or you can just make a simple serpent. Lay your snake flat on the ground in an S shape or try elevating the segments with some stakes. Be sure to visit a pumpkin patch or farmer's market to get a good price on a large quantity of pumpkins—you'll need at least ten.

Look What Just Slithered onto Your Front Porch

1. **SORT** your pumpkins from smallest to largest. After figuring out what position your serpent is going to be in on your lawn, **PUT** the largest pumpkin in the middle of the snake and the two littlest on either end. **ARRANGE** the rest of pumpkins in between, with them getting smaller as they reach each end.

2. If you want to, **CARVE** a pattern on each pumpkin. To create my diamondback pattern, I simply carved a diamond on the side of each pumpkin. (Take a look at some pictures of serpents and snakes for more pattern ideas.)

3 Make the butternut squash into the head of the snake by first **SLICING** the skin off the squash, then **CARVING** an evil eye and a nostril on each side. **CARVE** a mouth line, then **SLICE** the squash away in a V to make the mouth hang open.

4 **PUT** the carrot at the very end of the snake, to serve as its tail.

5 If you'd like to pose your serpent like a dragon, **INSERT** the stakes into the pumpkins and stick them in the ground to elevate the snake, roller-coaster fashion, to form hills.

EXTREME PUMPKIN FACTS

THINGS YOU PROBABLY NEVER KNEW ABOUT YOUR JACK-O'-LANTERN

Once upon a time in Central America, pumpkins were used as a holistic remedy for curing snake-bites. Here are some other facts about pumpkins I thought you should know:

- One acre of land—about the size of a football field without the end zones—can produce 20,000 pounds of pumpkins. That same amount of land can produce 42,800 pounds of strawberries, 36,700 pounds of potatoes, or one McMansion.

- Pumpkins originate in the Americas and have been around since 3500 B.C.

- The biggest pumpkin ever grown weighed in at 1,689 pounds.

- Pumpkin flowers are edible. But I don't recommend them—bluck!

- In North America, 80 percent of the pumpkins grown are available in October.

- Illinois is the leading pumpkin-producing state, with 90 to 95 percent of processed pumpkins being grown there. My home state of Michigan is number two.

- Pumpkin can be used as an exfoliant. I am not sure what an exfoliant is, but I know it makes your soap cost more.

MOHAWK PUMPKIN

YOU MIGHT NOT KNOW IT, BUT FARMERS ARE AN EXPERIMENTAL LOT. Farming is boring, so they try to liven things up by bringing new things to market. This year, my pumpkin guy was selling a large number of pumpkins with cracks in their skin. He didn't know what had caused the cracks, but he suspected it was the heavy rains in the early part of the growing season. Once it dried up again, the cracks healed, leaving ugly pumpkins with lots of blemishes. I loved them. These pumpkins were perfect for my Mohawk Pumpkin. I've done mohawks before, using carrots or candy corn for hair, and visitors to my website have sent me photos of pumpkins with mohawks made of sod, straw, and even scallions. This Mohawk Pumpkin is made with the head of a garage broom, and also features something new: three-dimensional teeth.

A Killer Mohawk, No Hairspray Necessary

YOU'LL NEED

- **1 pumpkin** *(preferably a crazy-looking one)*

- **CARVING AND GUTTING TOOLS: jigsaw, big metal spoon, Dremel tool with a square bit**

  NOTE: Power tools are optional. *(Substitute a square-tipped chisel for the Dremel tool. See The Standard Toolbox: Alternatives to Power Tools, page 9.)*

- **Dry erase marker**

- **The head of a broom, some carrots, or something else to make the mohawk**

- **Light**

1. **GUT** your pumpkin from the bottom.

2. **DRAW** a silly face—including the outline of each of the teeth—on the pumpkin and **CUT OUT** its eyes and nose (if it has one).

3. Begin **CARVING** the mouth by **CUTTING** away all of the space between the upper and lower teeth. Using your carving tool, **CUT** between the teeth—almost like flossing with a power tool—but don't go all the way through the pumpkin shell. A depth of about 1 inch (2.5 cm) should do the trick. Horizon-

tally, the canyons between the teeth should be at their narrowest about two-thirds of the way up the tooth from the jawline.

4. **SHAPE** the teeth further by carving away material from the front of each tooth. **CARVE** away more material at the top and base of each tooth, making it proudest at its widest point—two-thirds of the way up from the jaw-line. Remember to make some of the teeth different shapes than others. Don't rule out eye teeth, fangs, cavities, and some snaggleteeth to give your Mohawk Pumpkin some personality.

5. Next up is the hair transplant. If the material for your mohawk is widest at the bottom, like my broom or a bunch of carrots, **INSTALL** it from the inside by **CUTTING** a hole in the pumpkin that is slightly smaller than the widest part of your hairpiece, then pushing the Mohawk up through the hole from the inside. **JAM** it through there good, and it should stay in place.

6. If your mohawk is narrower (or the same size) at the bottom, like a flowerpot or some sod plugs, then **INSTALL** the mohawk from the outside by **CUTTING** a hole in the pumpkin that is slightly smaller than the narrowest part of your hair-piece, then slice away until the hairpiece fits when put in from the top. Gravity should help keep it in place.

7. **ILLUMINATE** your pumpkin with one of the methods described on page 11 or even a strobe light, and crank up the punk rock.

PUNK ALERT

HOW TO DEAL WITH TEENAGE TRICK-OR-TREATERS

I have nothing against teenage punks. But teenage punks on Halloween? I do anything I can to keep them away from my house. Whether they're up to trouble or are just trolling for candy, they're unwelcome. These greedy young adults should just buy their own candy and eat it in their parents' basement! Here are a handful of tricks sure to keep the teenagers away.

- First things first: Keep the garden hose handy. Not to rinse splattered eggs and shaving cream away, but to spray at the teenagers. The colder it is outside the better.

- Stock up on ketchup and hot sauce packets from your local fast-food restaurant. When teenagers come to the door looking for candy, smile and act like you are putting candy in their pillowcases, but slip in the packets instead. For added effect, open the packets first.

- Put a shop-vac near your front door. When teenagers ring the bell, open the door as quickly as possible and shove the vacuum hose inside their bags. Suck up as much candy as possible. Booyah!

FRIDAY THE 13TH
PUMPKIN

I NEVER CARED MUCH FOR THOSE SICKLY WHITE PUMPKINS UNTIL I STARTED WORKING ON THIS BOOK.

White pumpkins always reminded me of Casper the Friendly Ghost, who I can't stand because he isn't scary at all. But in the name of research, I bought a few white pumpkins and kicked them around the garage for a while. I kicked one of them so many times that it started to develop dents and scars. That ugly white pumpkin started to appeal to me in the same way that three-legged dogs do. But what to do with it? Eventually I realized a pumpkin of Jason Voorhees, the notorious killer from the *Friday the 13th* movies, would be killer. Apparently Jason's hockey mask was a Detroit Red Wings mask from the 1950s. I live in Detroit, which gave me extra incentive to add the red hash marks. I suggest you do the same.

On Friday the 13th, Nothing Will Save You!

YOU'LL NEED

- **1 white pumpkin** *(readily available in most pumpkin patches)*

- **CARVING TOOLS: jigsaw, steak knife, saw, big metal spoon**

  NOTE: Power tools are optional. *(See The Standard Toolbox: Alternatives to Power Tools, page 9.)*

- **1 orange pumpkin the same size as the white pumpkin** *(optional)*

- **Drill with a ³⁄₈-inch bit**

- **A few lengths of stiff wire,** *2 to 3 inches (5–7.5 cm) long*

- **Red permanent marker**

1. **CARVE** the white pumpkin to look like Jason's hockey mask by **CARVING** or **DRILLING** eye holes and **DRILLING** holes in a hockey-mask pattern. The holes above the eyes should form a squared-off U shape.

2. **SLICE** the entire front of the white pumpkin off. You now have a Jason Voorhees hockey mask made from a pumpkin. If this is all you want, you can skip to step 6.

3. **SLICE** a chunk off the front of the orange pumpkin that matches the size of your Jason mask and **GUT** the orange pumpkin.

4. See how the Jason mask fits on the orange pumpkin. You may need to slice more pumpkin off the mask or the orange pumpkin to get them to fit together better.

5. **LOOP** the lengths of wire through some of the mask holes and stick them into the flesh of the orange pumpkin to attach the mask to the head.

6. **DRAW** the red hash marks on the front of the mask.

7. **HIDE** the pumpkin someplace dark and spooky, and **WATCH** as it freaks out Halloween visitors.

TOO LAME TO LOATHE

THE TEN WORST HORROR MOVIE VILLAINS IN HISTORY

Jason Voorhees was such a great villain he inspired ten sequels. But here are ten movies featuring villains we will hopefully never see again.

1) *Killdozer* (1974). A bulldozer strikes a buried meteor and becomes possessed with the soul of an alien. (In case it's not clear, the bulldozer is the villain in this one.)

2) *Robot Monster* (1953). Features some guy wearing a gorilla suit with a diving helmet on his head. Somehow, this makes him a robot.

3) *The Stuff* (1985). The villain? Best described as whipped cream that eats your soul.

4) *The Mangler* (1995). A demonically possessed laundry-folding machine is the arch-nemesis in this flick. Seriously.

5) *Death Bed* (1977). Stars a waterbed that is filled with acid so that it can eat anyone stupid enough to hop aboard.

6) *Piranha 2* (1981). It's radioactive; it flies; it's a piranha!

7) *Jack Frost* (1996). Features a psychotic snowman in a movie that's even worse than the Michael Keaton flick of the same name.

8) *Basket Case* (1982). A post-op conjoined twin who didn't get any of the good parts when he was separated is understandably angry. How they thought of this plot is beyond even my twisted imagination.

9) *Leprechaun* (1993). The bad guy is a cheap leprechaun who will kill you for taking any of his gold. Don't miss the fifth movie in this series: *Leprechaun in the Hood*. On second thought—do.

10) *Night of the Lepus* (1972). A movie about giant killer rabbits. The special-effects magic includes closeups of real, live bunnies in slow motion.

FRANKEN-PUMPKIN

THE FRANKENPUMPKIN IS A HODGEPODGE OF EVERYTHING I HAVE EVER CREATED. Like Dr. Frankenstein (or *Pump*enstein), I am an impulsive creator—that is, I use whatever is close by. If I'm working on a new deck, it's likely that the support beams came from the roof of the garage. If I'm building a crib, you may not want to sleep on the fold-out bed tonight. I'm always stealing from one project to finish another, and the FrankenPumpkin does just that. Not using your basketball for a few days? Why not hack it up? How about that colander? Does your custom van have one of those bubble windows? Got a watermelon handy? Use what you've got. It will make a great FrankenPumpkin.

YOU'LL NEED

- **At least 1 pumpkin** *(possibly more)*

- **CARVING AND GUTTING TOOLS: jigsaw, steak knife, big metal spoon**

  NOTE: Power tools are optional. *(See The Standard Toolbox: Alternatives to Power Tools, page 9.)*

- **Some FrankenParts** *(see sidebar for ideas)*

- **Scissors,** *and anything needed to cut your FrankenParts*

- **Drill with a 3/8-inch bit**

- **Strong glue** *(to adhere stuff to the pumpkin)*

- **Soldering wire** *(which is easy to cut and looks cool), or staples, wire, or rawhide (for stitching)*

- **Paper** *(for tracing)*

- **Dry erase marker**

- **Two 1½ x 2-inch (about 4 x 5 cm) bolts** *(optional)*

- **More time on your hands than normal people**

Gives a Whole New Meaning to the Term "Pumpkin Patch"

1 **CUT** open and **GUT** your pumpkin from the top or bottom.

2 **GATHER** all of your FrankenParts together and **DECIDE** what your FrankenPumpkin will look like. You may want to make a sketch (see sidebar for tips).

THIN STUFF

3 Anything thinner than the skin of your pumpkin—like a colander, sheet metal, or fabric—can be placed on top of the pumpkin flesh. **CUT** a hunk of your material and **LAY** it over the pumpkin. If you are happy with how it looks, trace its shape on the pumpkin. If it doesn't fit well, try to either **RESHAPE** the material or **CARVE** away some of the pumpkin underneath it.

4 If you need to, **CUT** any eyes, nostrils, or mouth sections into the foreign material now.

5. **DRILL** holes every inch (2.5 cm) or so along the edge of the material. **DRILL** corresponding holes on your pumpkin, just outside the line you traced.

6. **GLUE** the material to the pumpkin, and then use the drilled holes to **THREAD** in the soldering wire. You don't have to actually sew the pieces together—a small amount of glue and a few pieces of wire will hold them in place. It's not like your pumpkin will be running through the village. It's just going to sit there.

THICK STUFF

7. To attach anything that's just as thick as or thicker than your pumpkin's skin, like the flesh of another pumpkin, you'll have to remove chunks of your pumpkin. **CUT** out some of your thick stuff; put it on a piece of paper.

8. **TRACE** the outline of the part onto the paper, then **CUT** the paper to make a pattern. **LAY** your pattern over the pumpkin. If you are happy with how it appears to fit, **TRACE** the pattern onto the pumpkin's skin.

9. **CARVE** away the pumpkin flesh in the shape of the pattern. If you need to, **CUT** any eyes, nostrils, or mouth sections into the foreign material.

10. **DRILL** holes every inch (2.5 cm) or so along the edge of the material, and corresponding holes along the edge of the pumpkin. **GLUE** and **STITCH** the material to the pumpkin as in step 6.

11. Once you have all your FrankenParts fastened to your pumpkin, **DRAW** and then **CARVE** the remainder of the face. **INSTALL** the bolts in the lower sides of the pumpkin to give it an authentic Frankenstein look, and **YELL**, "It's alive!"

RECYLED PUMPKIN

WHAT FRANKENPARTS WORK BEST?

Rounded parts are the best choice, as they will fit in the curvature of your FrankenPumpkin better. If an item is not rounded, use only a small hunk of it. Also, your pumpkin will be easier to assemble if items do not overlap.

- **Balls:** basket, soccer, rugby, foot, exercise, medicine, volley (avoid smaller balls like tennis or golf)

- **Anything that is a half-sphere:** colanders, plastic mixing bowls, R2D2's head, satellite dishes

- **Other large fruit:** watermelon, cantaloupe, gourds, and other pumpkins (especially white and green ones)

- **Things that add to the pumpkin's features:** wigs, sunglasses, Mr. Potatohead parts

- **Industrial-looking stuff:** nuts, bolts, wires, lights, lasers for a mad scientist finish

SUBURBAN NIGHTMARE PUMPKIN

AFTER I WROTE THE FIRST EXTREME PUMPKINS BOOK, MY WIFE GAVE BIRTH TO TWINS. This brought our spawn count up to three, requiring us to move into a bigger home. The new house has all the stuff people like: a spacious family room, a two-car garage, and even a white picket fence. I can hear you now: "The king of slash and burn lives in a house with a white picket fence?!" I know, it's bad for my image. Not to mention, not very effective: What trespasser couldn't leap a thigh-high barrier? That's why I decided to dress up our sweet little picket fence with this dripping, oozing, half-rotten pumpkin skull. It's much more effective at keeping out intruders and lets the neighbors know that the suburbs can't tame *this* guy.

If This Doesn't Say "No Trespassing," What Will?

YOU'LL NEED

- 1 butternut squash
- Dry erase marker
- **CARVING TOOLS:**
  jigsaw, angle grinder, steak knife

  NOTE: Power tools are optional.
  *(See The Standard Toolbox:
  Alternatives to Power Tools,
  page 9.)*

- **Drill with a hole saw attachment**
  *(it should be large enough to fit
  over your fence post)*

- **A fence** *with pointed slats, a large
  stake, or a sharpened stick*

1. **DRAW** the eyes, nose, and mouth on the squash.
   I decided to go with aviator sunglass–shaped eyes.

2. **TURN** your butternut squash on its side to carve
   the jawline. Beginning 1 to 2 inches (1.5–5 cm) below where the mouth will be, **CUT** a horizontal line
   to create the bottom of the chin. Cut from the center of the chin up at an angle toward the back of the
   squash, then turn the saw and cut toward where
   the ear would be. Just before you reach where the
   ear would be, turn the saw again and cut out
   through the back of the squash, where the spine
   would attach to the skull. A large chunk of squash
   should fall away, and your creation will really start
   looking skullish.

3 For the mouth itself, pretend you are a reconstructive dentist and do your best (or worst?) work **CARVING** the teeth. The teeth should be recessed a little farther than you may think initially, because you'll be removing the skin of the squash.

4 Now **CARVE** out the eyes and nose.

5 **SHAVE** off the skin of the squash (optional but worth it!). You'll find that a butternut squash has a network of greenish veins under the skin, adding to your Suburban Nightmare Pumpkin's creepiness.

6 **DRILL** a hole all the way through the squash from bottom to top. Don't worry about keeping the drill straight, as a little tilt makes it look even more brutal.

7 **PLACE** the skull on the fence, stake, or sharpened stick. In a day or two it will attract birds, bugs, and all sorts of horrid critters. A strong, sunny day can provide enough radiation to give it a parched appearance as well. **ENJOY** as your neighbors stare at your once beautiful picket fence in disgust.

PUMPKIN PRANK
ROASTED BUTTERNUT SQUASH SKULLS

If you're hosting a Halloween dinner party, nothing looks more inviting on a platter than a couple of roasted skulls. Here are some tips for cooking up some of the butternut squash variety.

1) Carefully CLEAN all of your pumpkin carving tools. You can put most saw blades in the dishwasher. If washing by hand, be very careful, as it can be a dicey (er, slicey) operation.

2) SKIN the squashes, CARVE skeletal faces, and BRUSH with melted butter. SPRINKLE with salt and pepper. (Did I just use the word sprinkle?)

3) ROAST at 400 degrees Fahrenheit (204 degrees Celcius) for about 1 hour, or until tender. There should be little resistance when you STAB the skulls with a knife.

4) SERVE your squash skulls on a big platter, perhaps with paper collars, or slice them vertically then horizontally and insert toothpicks à la *Hellraiser*. However you present them, some of your guests won't eat them. But that's their loss— it's just squash, after all.

CRO-MAGNON PUMPKIN

I LOVE GOING TO THE PUMPKIN PATCH AFTER MOST OF THE PUMPKINS HAVE BEEN SENT OFF TO MARKET. Pumpkin growers pick all of the best-looking, perfectly round pumpkins to sell, leaving behind all of the misshapen, deformed ones. So if you're looking for a pumpkin that is more than half green, it's right there. Pimply? Check. Dented? Got it. Strange? Oh, yeah. For me, spotting an ugly pumpkin is like cloud-gazing. But while clouds always look like animals or Disney characters, ugly pumpkins all look like hideous beasts. In this pumpkin's case, I immediately saw the skull of a Cro-Magnon man. Abrasion, limited space (that dent is from the wire fence it grew under), and plenty of food and water had made it the biggest, ugliest pumpkin I had ever seen—180 pounds (81 kg)! I had to have it. If you ever find an equally hideous pumpkin, I suggest you buy it too.

Halloween Is Like Valentine's Day for the Ugly

YOU'LL NEED

- **The biggest, ugliest, and dented-est pumpkin you can find**

- **Dry erase marker**

- **CARVING AND GUTTING TOOLS:** reciprocating saw, angle grinder, steak knife, big metal spoon

  NOTE: **Power tools are optional.** *(See The Standard Toolbox: Alternatives to Power Tools, page 9.)*

- **A towel and a friend** *to help lift the pumpkin (or just lots of muscles and a strong back)*

- **A powerful light source** *(Big pumpkins demand big effects. A spotlight or work light will do nicely.)*

1. To **MOVE** your huge pumpkin to your workspace, lay a towel down next to it. **ROLL** the pumpkin onto the center of the towel and **LIFT** one corner while having a friend lift the other. Voilà! It moves easily.

2. Before carving your pumpkin, **DRAW** an ugly face on it. The key to a Cro-Magnon Pumpkin is the teeth. Your jack-o'-lantern should have either a larger-than-normal number of teeth, or very few. No matter which you choose, the teeth should be strangely shaped and cavity-ridden.

3. **CARVE** and **GUT** your pumpkin. If they are large enough, you can gut your pumpkin through its gaping eye sockets. When you carve the teeth, taper them by rounding off each corner. Make a receding gum line by **FLAYING** the skin of the teeth at the gum line: Use an angle grinder to strip off the outer layer of the pumpkin skin, starting at a depth of 3/8 inch (1 cm) and going deeper as necessary. **FLAY** your Cro-Magnon around the eye sockets as well for extra effect.

4. Use a spotlight to **ILLUMINATE** the cranial cavity brighter than any Cro-Magnon brain ever did.

EXTREMELY DEFORMED

WHAT TO MAKE WITH THE REST OF THOSE LOSER PUMPKINS

Making a huge, dented pumpkin into a primitive man isn't the only thing to do with unpretty pumpkins. Here are more loser pumpkins and the fantastic creations you can make from them.

- **Pimply Pumpkin.** Make a tormented teen nerd. If you don't have any photos of nerds to work from, write to me, and I'll send you one of me in 1987. I was the coolest guy in AV club.

- **Dented-on-One-Side Pumpkin.** Use the dent to your advantage by placing a boot next to, or a sledgehammer into, the dent to make it look like your jack-o'-lantern has just received a pounding.

- **Green Pumpkin.** An unripe pumpkin is perfect for certain themes. Seasickness? Radiation exposure? Food poisoning? You decide.

- **White Pumpkin.** White pumpkins make excellent skulls (and Jason masks; see page 60). One great thing about white pumpkins is the luminous glow you get from them when they're lit—they're much more translucent than their orange counterparts. Use a green bulb inside for an eerie effect.

- **Squat Pumpkin.** If your pumpkin is much shorter than it is wide, try putting an empty box (or something else) on top of it to make it appear as though it was crushed in a moving accident.

Complete the scene by giving the victim a pained expression.

- **Tall Pumpkin.** Every once in a while I put my head in a jack-o'-lantern and walk around. Most of the time, the gag is just OK. When you use an extra-tall pumpkin, though, the stunt gets the reaction you want. You can position the mouth so that you can see out of it and the tall pumpkin adds quite a few inches to your height.

- **Cracked Pumpkin.** Some pumpkins develop cracks as they grow. Put knives in the cracks for a gruesome, stabbed-in-the-head effect.

- **Moldy Pumpkin.** Moldy pumpkins look a little bit like old men—they turn white, their skin gets wrinkly, and their eye sockets tend to turn inward. Why not add inexpensive glasses, a hat, a coffee mug, and a cigar to complete the caricature?

- **Giant-Stemmed Pumpkin.** If you have a pumpkin with a huge stem, you can turn it on its side and use the stem as a nose.

- **Conjoined Pumpkins.** Finding two pumpkins that grew from one stem is rare, but it does happen. Grab that pumpkin quick! And use it to make some Siamese twins.

FULL-DIAPER PUMPKIN

FOR THIS, MY SECOND OPUS ON PUMPKIN CARVING, I wanted to include a pumpkin that represented the most terrifying thing I could think of. As a parent (of twins), I can tell you that nothing is more frightening than a morning confrontation with an overflowing diaper. You might not think it sounds so scary, but trust me, the thought that one of your squirming little children may have spent the night spreading his waste all over the bedroom is the stuff of nightmares.

Guess What? It's Your Turn to Babysit

YOU'LL NEED

- **1 long, narrow pumpkin** (or butternut squash)

- **Pumpkin guts** (from just 1 pumpkin will do, but 2 or 3 pumpkins' worth works best)

- **CARVING AND GUTTING TOOLS: jigsaw, steak knife, big metal spoon**

   NOTE: Power tools are optional. (See The Standard Toolbox: Alternatives to Power Tools, page 9.)

- **Dry erase marker**

- **A diaper**

- **Duct tape**

- **Doll arms and legs**

- **Glue**

1. **CUT** open your pumpkin at the bottom of its back and **GUT** it, saving all the goop you pull out.

2. On the top half of the front of your pumpkin, **DRAW** and then **CARVE** a crying-baby face. Babies have big eyes, little round nostrils, and no more than a couple of teeth. Babies cry . . . a lot. Oh, man, do babies cry a lot. Make sure your Full-Diaper Pumpkin has a big, crying mouth.

3. **PLACE** your newborn wonder someplace fun, like the bassinet or dinner table.

4. **FILL** the diaper with lots of pumpkin guts.

5. Find a crafty way to **ATTACH** the diaper to the back of the pumpkin. I used duct tape. A staple gun would probably work too, but stapling a diaper to a baby is wrong on many levels.

6. **GLUE** the doll arms and legs to the sides of the pumpkin. Helpfully **INFORM** your wife that something smells funny.

THE ULTIMATE PUMPKIN-CARVING PARTY

There's no better way to get in the Halloween spirit—and show off your mad carving skills—than by throwing a pumpkin-carving party. Below are some tips for making your party truly legendary.

- **Plenty of Pumpkins:** Provide the pumpkins for your guests. This not only saves everyone else a trip to the pumpkin patch, but offers you the chance to fill some of the pumpkins with pennies or fake blood (see Pumpkin Pranks, pages 31 and 51).

- **Carving Zone:** Designate a carving area by laying out a plastic drop cloth. Better yet, hold your pumpkin-carving party out-of-doors, where everyone can make a mess. (If it rains, you can always move into the garage.)

- **Tools (Including Kid-Friendly Ones):** If you don't have enough carving tools for everyone, ask your guests to bring theirs. Most pumpkin-carving tools sold in stores feature dull blades and plastic handles that are perfect for older children and pre-teens. Skip the power tools: They're not a good idea at a party with lots of young (or tipsy) guests. Offer your guests an assortment of gutting implements. Kitchen tools such as ice cream scoops, serving spoons, and stir-fry spatulas will all do the job—goop removal is not an exact science, after all. Provide markers for very young kids, so they can design their pumpkins and then have adults do the carving.

- **Guts Disposal:** Have at least one large trash receptacle ready (or more if you have a lot of people coming) for carvers to put their pumpkin parts and guts in. Keep a pack of wet wipes on hand for post–pumpkin massacre cleanup.

- **Spooky Snack Contest:** Each year at our party, we hold a contest for the best "spooky snack." Past winners include ghoulish cupcakes, grave-yard pies, and even a skull covered with lunch-meat. See page 71 for instructions on making a roasted butternut squash skull. Since most people don't seem to like eating skulls (whether they are roasted or covered with lunchmeat), provide your guests with pizza, chips and dip, cupcakes, and other kid-friendly party treats.

- **Pumpkin Punch Bowl:** A pumpkin also makes a decent punch bowl. Slice one in half, carefully scrape the sides, and line it with plastic wrap. Voilà! A unique serving vessel.

- **Pumpkin Piñata:** Since normal piñatas just aren't strong enough to stand up to an adult whacking, a pumpkin full of candy would be a pretty cool substitute.

- **End with Extreme Pyrotechnics:** I like to end the party with a grand pumpkin finale. Usually I pull out a giant pumpkin and light it up with a fun pyrotechnique. If your stunt is great enough, you'll be a hero until you do it again next year.

DOLL-EATER PUMPKIN

NO DISCUSSION OF DOLLS IS COMPLETE WITHOUT SOMEONE MENTIONING that most dolls are out of proportion to how a real woman looks. I'll spare you. Let's talk instead about the difference between brand-name dolls and no-name dolls. Our poor friend in this photo is a brand-name doll (generously donated by my niece), and I could have used a no-name facsimile in my pumpkin art for one-tenth the price. Unfortunately, if you want to disturb your audience, you have to crush and maim something other people hold dear. After you create a piece like this one, you can only hope that a serious doll collector stops by your place on Halloween. "Is that what I think it is?" he or she will ask. To which you can respond, "Yeah, it's a limited edition. It was new-in-box before I used it for this project." That ought to scare 'em.

From Fashion Victim to Death by Pumpkin

YOU'LL NEED

- 1 fairly large pumpkin

- **CARVING AND GUTTING TOOLS:** jigsaw, steak knife, big metal spoon

  NOTE: Power tools are optional. *(See The Standard Toolbox: Alternatives to Power Tools, page 9.)*

- **A fashion doll** *or other victim*

- **Black marker**

- **FAKE BLOOD:** 8 ounces corn syrup, 12 drops red food coloring, 1 teaspoon cornstarch, 1 drop blue food coloring *(optional)*

1. **CUT** open and **GUT** your pumpkin.

2. **SLICE** and dice until you have created a mean, hungry face. Give it fangs and angry eyes. This pumpkin is out for blood!

3. Use the marker to **DRAW** a dead expression on your fashion doll's face.

4. **LEAVE** your victim for dead inside the pumpkin's mouth.

5. **MIX** the fake blood ingredients and **DOUSE** the victim's torso with it to make the scene a true bloodbath.

JACK-O'-LANTERN SNACKS

OTHER THINGS PUMPKINS LOOK COOL EATING

You've fed him a pretty dolly, but your jack-o'-lantern is still hungry. Here are some other things that might satisfy his huge appetite.

- **A Limb:** Try one of those fake hands or legs that are sold at novelty shops or Halloween stores.

- **Meaty Bones:** Ask your butcher if he has a bone you can buy. Something large and meaty will look extra cool.

- **Tons of Candy:** Halloween is all about the candy, so why not put some in your pumpkin's mouth?

- **A Smaller Pumpkin:** Spread the news that pumpkins are cannibals. This gimmick also makes a great front cover for your first book.

- **Your Pet:** It will be hard to get your dog or cat to stay in your pumpkin's mouth all night, but you can snap a good photo of Fido or Socks being eaten by a jack-o'-lantern. Just put his food dish inside the pumpkin and ready your camera.

- **A Skull:** Pumpkins aren't afraid of humans! Most Halloween stores sell plastic skulls that won't fail to disturb upright onlookers.

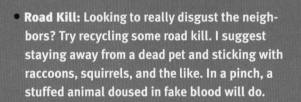

- **Road Kill:** Looking to really disgust the neighbors? Try recycling some road kill. I suggest staying away from a dead pet and sticking with raccoons, squirrels, and the like. In a pinch, a stuffed animal doused in fake blood will do.

BOOGER-EATING PUMPKIN

DOES EVERY KID EAT THEIR BOOGERS? I don't think so, but my friend Brad says they do. It is a bad topic for us; it has almost ended our friendship. Brad swears everyone has eaten their boogers, even me. I swear I always knew it was gross and have never done it. I see booger-eating as a disgusting act that I've spent my entire life avoiding. The only problem is, I consider myself pretty worldly. I like to think that I've experienced almost everything—I've flown in balloons, climbed mountains, fallen in love, traveled the world, and even jumped out of an airplane. I have done it all . . . except taste boogers. And now I'm wondering what they must taste like. At least I can live vicariously through this jack-o'-lantern.

Embrace Your Inner Snot-Eater

YOU'LL NEED

- **1 pumpkin with a flat or turned-in face** *(an odd texture and/or color will help add to the "schoolyard outcast" look)*

- **Dry erase marker**

- **CARVING AND GUTTING TOOLS: jigsaw, big metal spoon**

  NOTE: Power tools are optional. *(See The Standard Toolbox: Alternatives to Power Tools, page 9.)*

- **Can of Great Stuff, or another expanding foam insulation**

- **Work gloves**

- **1 large piece of cardboard**

1 **CUT** open and **GUT** your pumpkin.

2 **DRAW** and then **CARVE** a face on your pumpkin. The secret is the expression—booger-eaters disgust themselves by the act that they are committing, so capture their angst with a misshapen mouth full of crooked teeth. Make one nostril larger than the other—experienced booger-eaters know that you only get snot from one side at a time.

3 **READ** the directions on your can of foam insulation. For this step, you'll need to use the gloves, because if you get insulation on your skin it will take forever to get off. **LAY** your pumpkin face up on the cardboard and squirt a trail of insulation from inside one nostril, out onto the face, and into the mouth. It doesn't take much insulation to make it work. (You can use the remaining insulation to mold something. Spray it on a large piece of cardboard, and once it dries, carve it using a knife or rotary tool. Expert costume-makers use this stuff all the time.)

 WAIT for the insulation to dry before moving your pumpkin. It will take a couple of hours. In the meantime, resist the urge to touch the goop; it is really sticky.

GIVE this pumpkin to anyone who has a four-year-old.

BOOGERS 101

MORE THAN YOU EVER WANTED TO KNOW

Since boogers play such a huge role in this book—and in our lives—I thought I'd share some booger facts with you.

- For the record, *booger* is the technical term for dried-up snot mixed with dust, pollen, and anything else in the air.

- I know this is disgusting, but the average person swallows a quart (almost 1 L) of mucus every day.

- If swallowing your own snot isn't disgusting enough, you can buy a product called a nasal aspirator, which is like a long straw you can use to get babies' snot out of their noses. (Very disgusting until you spend a sleepless night with a stuffy-nosed baby. Trust me, the stuffy nose does not keep them from crying.)

- Most animals, such as cows, horses, and dogs, simply remove their own snot with their tongues. But human babies apparently don't possess this skill.

- Since your boogers are mostly dust, you'll notice that if you spend the day welding, your boogers will look like welding slag, and if you spend the day sawing cedar lumber, you'll have fragrant brown-red boogers. This analogy can be applied to any dust-producing activity.

- In 2002, a truly tasteless company produced booger-flavored jelly beans. Four of five children said they tasted just like real boogers.

GODZILLA PUMPKIN

SEEKING TO BUILD THE ULTIMATE IN PUMPKIN YARD ART THIS HALLOWEEN? I bet you are. After all, you're reading a book called *Extreme Pumpkins II*. Maybe the first book wasn't extreme enough for you, or maybe you feel that anything dumb that's worth doing is worth doing to excess. Either way, I like your style, kiddo. Here's how to make the granddaddy of all extreme pumpkin displays: the Godzilla Pumpkin. Don't be intimidated by the fact that you need a pumpkin patch full of squashes to build this four-foot-tall monster. Once you're done, your front yard will be the most impressive one on the block.

YOU'LL NEED

- **1 Hubbard squash** *(for the head)*

- **CARVING TOOLS:**
  jigsaw, steak knife, angle grinder

  NOTE: Power tools are optional.
  (See The Standard Toolbox: Alternatives to Power Tools, page 9.)

- **Drill** *with a bit just smaller than the diameter of your dowels*

- **12 feet (3.6 m) of wooden dowels** **½ inch (1.3 cm) in diameter**

- **1 large, tall pumpkin** *(for the torso)*

- **2 medium-sized pumpkins** *(for the legs)*

- **1 very large squash or gourd** *(for the tail)*

- **A bunch of pumpkin parts and scraps, or another large pumpkin** *(to make the feet, dorsal spikes, and arms)*

- **Cardboard and permanent markers**

- **A bunch of small pumpkins** *(to make into frightened citizens)*

- **Lighter fluid, a lighter, and a fire extinguisher** *(optional)*

Incredible, Unstoppable Titan of Terror!

HEAD

(1) On page 43, I describe how to make a Hubbard squash look like an alligator head. Godzilla has a head that looks like an alligator's. So go to page 43 and **CARVE** an alligator head already.

(2) To make the alligator mouth open, **CUT** along the mouth line. Then separate the lower jaw from the rest of the head by **CUTTING** downward from the back of the mouth.

(3) **SECURE** the mouth in an open position by lining it up where you want it and then **DRILLING** a hole in it and then a corresponding hole in the head. **CONNECT** the two pieces by placing a length of dowel half into the head hole and half into the lower jaw. In woodworking, this is called a dowel joint. If your dowel joint doesn't hold or just seems like a pain, substitute long deck screws (2 to 3 inches [5–7.5 cm]).

TORSO

(4) The torso is fairly simple. Just get out your large, tall pumpkin, and **CARVE** a large oval with some horizontal lines through it for Godzilla's stomach plates. You can also just **CARVE** the outline of the oval and the lines. Then **REMOVE** the stem.

LEGS AND TAIL

(5) The legs and tail make a sort of tripod that holds up the entire operation, so it's important to secure them to each other well. **POSITION** the leg pumpkins next to each other, with the tail squash between them. **CUT** three lengths of dowel. You want them to be as long as possible (without being longer than the pumpkins), to make the base as sturdy as possible.

(6) **HOLDING** the legs and tail in place, **CONNECT** the right and left leg, the right leg and tail, and the left leg and tail with dowel joints. If the arrangement is not stable enough to place the torso on, **CUT** some more dowels and shore it up.

FEET AND ARMS

(7) Using either pumpkin scraps or a new pumpkin, **CUT** out some arms and feet. (I'll leave it up to you to decide what Godzilla arms and feet should look like.) **ATTACH** the arms using dowel joints (you can also use long deck screws). You don't need to attach the feet—just **PLACE** them on the ground in front of the legs.

DORSAL SPIKES

(8) Using your scrap pumpkin, **CUT** some dorsal spikes that are shaped sort of like maple leaves. **SECURE** them to the torso and tail using dowel joints (or long deck screws).

SETUP

 Now you are ready to set up your Godzilla. **PLACE** the legs and tail where you want them, and **REST** the torso on top. You may need to dowel-joint it in place. **PUT** the feet in front of the legs, and **REST** the head on top of the torso (you may need to dowel-joint that, too).

Beware: No pumpkin display is more likely to attract neighborhood teens with baseball bats than this Godzilla. It almost screams "Smash me!" If you are like me, you'll want to take "prevenge"—plan ahead to automatically get revenge. Prevenge could include hiding a steel skeleton in your Godzilla sure to break any baseball bat that tried to smash it. Prevenge also might include a garden sprinkler with a motion sensor to soak anyone who approaches your monster, or a 120-decibel pumpkin-theft alarm. Whatever method you dream up, prevenge will allow you to sleep with a big Cheshire cat smile, the sort of smile you used to have as a teen after smashing all the pumpkins in your neighborhood.

SCENERY

 Godzilla wouldn't be complete without some scenery to chew. **MAKE** some cardboard buildings to lay at Godzilla's feet. Use names of local businesses, friends, or party guests to add to the fun.

11 Little pumpkins make good frightened citizens. So they look good in photos, simply **DRAW** on their terrified faces with a marker and spread them around your cardboard town.

12 The more sedate among you will want to present your town as it looked **BEFORE** Godzilla arrived. Others will prefer to show how the town looked **AFTER** Godzilla had his way with it. If you are the carnage-loving sort, you can **HAVE FUN**. Once you've positioned your small pumpkin citizens, cardboard buildings, and other scenery, give your city a series of well-placed **STOMPS**. The path of destruction should **WIND** its way through the city so it looks like Godzilla (not you) is responsible.

GODZILLA UNDER THE MICROSCOPE

THE STRANGEST GODZILLA-MOVIE MONSTERS (NOT YET MADE INTO PUMPKINS)

Some of the Godzilla monsters are quite odd. I know that they were invented in Japan, but let's face it: Just because the world is getting smaller every day doesn't mean that every export is going to make sense around the globe. Here is my layman's analysis of some of the strangest creatures in the Godzilla movies.

- **Megalon:** Take an old Godzilla suit, replace the head with a bug's head, and then put some Earth-drilling equipment where the hands would be. Voilà! Megalon.

- **Mothra:** How does a freakin' moth stand a chance against a giant lizard? Moths eat leaves. Lizards eat moths. It just isn't convincing to me.

- **Jet Jaguar:** This robot might be cool if he didn't look like something from a 1980s heavy-metal video. His name stinks too. He doesn't look like a jet or a jaguar. A more descriptive name would be "Robo-Knight-Suit Jerk."

- **Biollante:** Part monster, part human, and part plant, this female monster doesn't get along with any of the other monsters. She also kind of looks pregnant, which makes me think the writer's wife was expecting when he thought up this mean-spirited monster.

- **Rodan:** A pterodactyl-looking monster who would be really effective if his opponents were bunny-rabbit monsters.

- **Space Godzilla:** A combination of Godzilla DNA and some space crystals, this guy is apparently as smart as a person, and this makes him a major threat. So I guess you could just distract him with a bad TV show and then kick his butt.

INDEX

SPECIAL THANKS

I would first like to thank my wife and family, for allowing me to spend the time to create this book. It wasn't easy to find the time with this one, so they deserve a special thanks. My wife is especially important, because she keeps all of the kids alive while I tinker in the garage. She's also a fine-looking woman.

Penguin Publishing has made me a bit of a Halloween star. Marian, Tom, and the gang not only made me a bestselling author, they put me on national TV. Most importantly, they made the experience of being an author an especially fun one. Also, they didn't press charges when I cut up the recycling bin in their office to make a last-minute Halloween costume.

The folks at Quirk Packaging are especially important. If you know me, you know that my work is pretty sloppy. Quirk makes it look presentable. Sarah, Lynne, Jennifer, and Sue, thanks.

The family and friends who cheer my pumpkin exploits also deserve thanks. They had to endure the cancellation of last year's pumpkin-carving party so that I could fly to New York for a last-minute TV appearance. Sorry about that.

Anyone who bought my prior book and anyone who is buying this one—thanks so much. Beyond the money, the idea that people want to read what I have to say is an amazing thing. I have tried to make this book interesting and fun.

And to the two Boy Scouts who proved themselves to be my number one fans by dragging their parents to both of my book signings: Thanks.

ABOUT THE AUTHOR

TOM NARDONE is the founder of ExtremePumpkins.com, an alternative pumpkin-carving website with a large and largely deranged following. His first book, *Extreme Pumpkins*, was a national bestseller that landed him on *Live with Regis & Kelly*, *Good Morning America Weekend*, and MTV's *TRL* (they are still removing the pumpkin pulp from their studios). He lives in the suburbs of Detroit with his wife and three kids where he runs an internet company.

The first word in Halloween.

Available wherever books are sold.

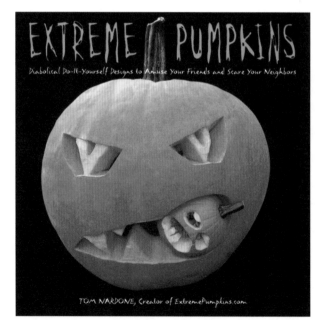